Where Germs Lurk

Writing, Simplifying, and Evaluating Expressions

Lori Barker

Consultants

Pamela Dase, M.A.Ed.
National Board Certified Teacher

Barbara Talley, M.S.
Texas A&M University

Publishing Credits

Dona Herweck Rice, *Editor-in-Chief*
Robin Erickson, *Production Director*
Lee Aucoin, *Creative Director*
Timothy J. Bradley, *Illustration Manager*
Sara Johnson, M.S.Ed., *Senior Editor*
Aubrie Nielsen, M.S.Ed., *Associate Education Editor*
Jennifer Kim, M.A.Ed., *Associate Education Editor*
Neri Garcia, *Senior Designer*
Stephanie Reid, *Photo Editor*
Rachelle Cracchiolo, M.S.Ed., *Publisher*

Image Credits

Teacher Created Materials

5301 Oceanus Drive
Huntington Beach, CA 92649-1030
http://www.tcmpub.com
ISBN 978-1-4333-3455-9
© 2012 Teacher Created Materials, Inc.

Table of Contents

What Are Germs?

"Cover your mouth when you cough!"

Sound familiar? We have all been told to cover our mouths when we cough or sneeze. You know to wash your hands after using the restroom and before eating, and not to put your mouth on a drinking fountain. We do these things to prevent the spread of germs. But what are germs anyway?

Germs are tiny, living things that you can only see with a microscope. They are **microbes**, or microorganisms (mahy-kroh-AWR-guh-niz-uhmz). Some germs are made up of only one cell. Others are not even a complete cell and need to be inside another living organism in order to survive.

Many microbes are necessary to help us stay healthy. Unfortunately there are germs that lurk all around us that can make us very sick.

Covering a cough or sneeze helps prevent the spread of germs. It is best not to use a bare hand to cover your mouth since germs are easily spread through contact with hands.

As much as we try to prevent the spread of germs, most people get sick once in awhile. Sometimes students must be absent from school due to illness. Schools keep track of students' absences by collecting data.

Numerical expressions can be used to help understand data. A numerical expression is a combination of numbers and operations that has not been **evaluated**. Suppose in Mr. Marin's fifth period class, there were twice as many absences as in his third period class. The numerical expression 2(46) represents the first semester absences from Mr. Marin's fifth period class.

First Semester Absences in Mr. Marin's Math Classes	
Class	**Number of Absences**
1st period	75
3rd period	46
5th period	2(46)

Different Ways to Show It

Multiplication expressions can be shown in different ways:

2 × 46   **2 • 46**

2(46)   **(2)(46)**

Louis Pasteur

When was the last time you had a cold? Colds are caused by germs. Louis Pasteur (LOO-ee pa-STUR) is known as the father of microbiology. He developed the "germ theory of disease." He found that microorganisms can cause disease, such as the last cold you had. He found that germs lurk in the air, on your skin, in your body, and just about anywhere else you can imagine.

Louis Pasteur (1822–1895) did a lot to help us understand germs.

Lurking Germs

Bacteria and **viruses** are two common types of microorganisms that can cause **infections**. Bacteria are small, but viruses are even smaller.

In 1865, great numbers of silkworms began dying in a town in France. The silkworms were not making their cocoons, so the silk industry was suffering. Pasteur was asked to study the silkworms to see what was causing their illness. When Pasteur looked at sick silkworms under a microscope, he saw microbes. The silkworms had germs that were making them sick.

Silkworms are not really worms. They are caterpillars.

The cocoons of silkworms are used to make silk.

Silkworms eat mulberry leaves.

In one of his experiments, Pasteur spread the remains of some sick silkworms onto leaves and fed the leaves to healthy silkworms. The healthy silkworms got sick. He spread the remains of some healthy silkworms onto leaves and fed those leaves to other healthy silkworms. This time, the healthy silkworms did not get sick.

Different Ways to Show It

Pasteur studied silkworms to figure out what was making them sick. Imagine that in one experiment he had 100 silkworms that he needed to divide into four groups. The numerical expression $\frac{100}{4}$ represents the number of silkworms in each group.

Division expressions can be shown in different ways:

$$4\overline{)100} \qquad \frac{100}{4} \qquad 100 \div 4$$

Only the healthy silkworms that ate the remains of sick silkworms became ill. Specific germs from the sick silkworms infected them. Pasteur saw with his microscope that germs were living on the sick silkworms. With this research, Pasteur made a clear connection between germs and disease.

Silk thread comes from the cocoons of silkworms. Dry cocoons are soaked in boiling water to soften them. Then the fibers are unwound to produce thread.

This silk thread will be dyed and woven into cloth.

Pasteurization

Germs can lurk in the foods we eat and the liquids we drink. Heat can kill germs. But too much heat can destroy whatever the germs are in. Pasteurization (pas-chuh-ruh-ZAY-shun) is a process that uses heat to kill germs without destroying the flavor and other properties of food. Louis Pasteur developed it. Food is heated below the **boiling point** for a certain amount of time. Today, milk and many other foods and drinks are pasteurized.

LET'S EXPLORE MATH

Here are some guidelines for pasteurizing milk:

Pasteurization Temperature	Heating Time
145°F (63°C)	30 minutes
162°F (72°C)	15 seconds
192°F (89°C)	1 second

a. Heating milk to 192°F instead of 162°F saves time. Write a numerical expression that shows the difference in the two temperatures.

b. A dairy factory pasteurizes its milk at 63°C. Write a numerical expression to show how many seconds it takes to pasteurize milk at that temperature. (*Hint:* Remember, 1 minute = 60 seconds)

c. The average dairy cow produces about 19,710 gallons of milk in one year (365 days). Write a numerical expression to find the number of gallons the average dairy cow produces each day.

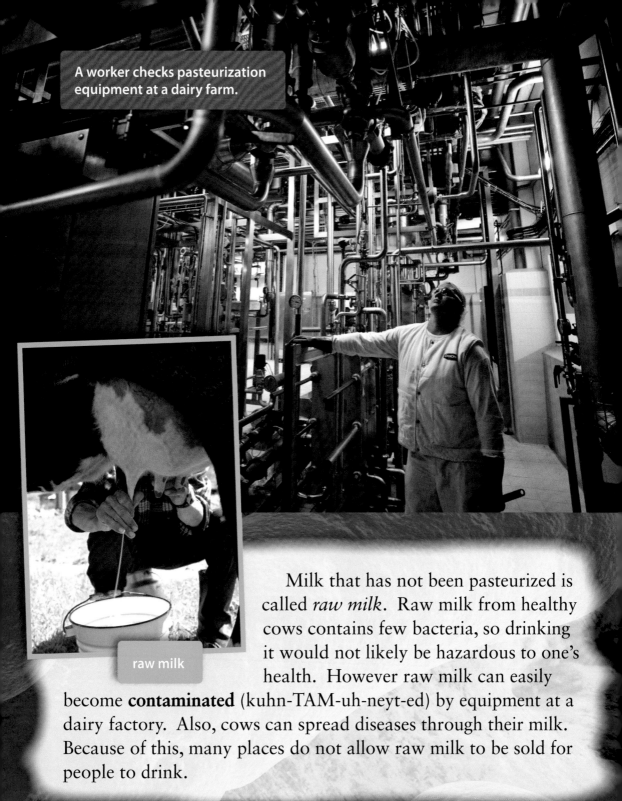

A worker checks pasteurization equipment at a dairy farm.

raw milk

Milk that has not been pasteurized is called *raw milk*. Raw milk from healthy cows contains few bacteria, so drinking it would not likely be hazardous to one's health. However raw milk can easily become **contaminated** (kuhn-TAM-uh-neyt-ed) by equipment at a dairy factory. Also, cows can spread diseases through their milk. Because of this, many places do not allow raw milk to be sold for people to drink.

Having a few disease-causing bacteria is typically not much of a threat. Our bodies are usually good at attacking such invaders. The problem is that germs can multiply quickly to become more than the body can fight.

Bacteria spread by making more of themselves. Each cell splits in half, which is the same as doubling. Look at how quickly one cell becomes many more.

1 cell doubles	$(1) \cdot 2 = 2$
2 cells double	$(2) \cdot 2 = 4$
4 cells double	$(2 \cdot 2) \cdot 2 = 8$
8 cells double	$(2 \cdot 2 \cdot 2) \cdot 2 = 16$
16 cells double	$(2 \cdot 2 \cdot 2 \cdot 2) \cdot 2 = 32$
32 cells double	$(2 \cdot 2 \cdot 2 \cdot 2 \cdot 2) \cdot 2 = 64$

When one cell multiplies and becomes two cells, it does so by dividing in half. Notice that multiplying by 2 gives the same result as dividing by $\frac{1}{2}$.

$$1 \cdot 2 = 2$$
$$1 \div \frac{1}{2} = 2$$

MRSA bacteria can multiply quickly.

Exponential Form

A factor that is multiplied two or more times (such as 3 • 3 • 3 • 3) can be written in **exponential form**. Exponential form has a **base** and an **exponent**. The base is the number used as a factor. The exponent is the number that tells how many equal factors must be multiplied. 3 • 3 • 3 • 3 is written 3^4 in exponential form. It is read *three to the fourth power*.

Did you notice that after four doublings, there are 16 cells? We can show this numerical expression in exponential form. Using exponents saves a lot of time and space when representing large numbers. The expression 2^4 represents 2 • 2 • 2 • 2, which equals 16. 2^4 shows that each time a cell multiplies, it creates two cells. Multiplying four times creates a total of 16 cells.

bacteria cells dividing

LET'S EXPLORE MATH

Imagine a bacteria cell that can create five of itself each time it splits.

a. Write an expression to find how many cells there would be after three splits. Use exponential form.

b. Write an expression to find how many cells there would be after six splits. Use exponential form.

Germs on Your Hands

Germs lurk on your hands. Did you wash your hands yesterday? How many times? The **variable** w can stand for the number of times you washed your hands. Variables are letters or symbols that can be used to represent numbers. This number may not be known. The number can also change or have different values at different times. Other letters such as x, y, and n are often used as variables. Even pictures or boxes can be variables.

You expect doctors to wash their hands before examining you. This became common only after many scientists, including Pasteur, argued for years that hand washing can prevent the spread of many diseases.

When you wash your hands, you need to use soap and warm water. Each wash should last at least 20 seconds. Multiply the number of times you wash your hands in a day by 20 seconds. You get the total amount of time you spend washing your hands in a day. We can show this as $20w$. This is an **algebraic** (al-juh-BREY-ik) **expression**. It is a combination of numbers, variables, and one or more operations.

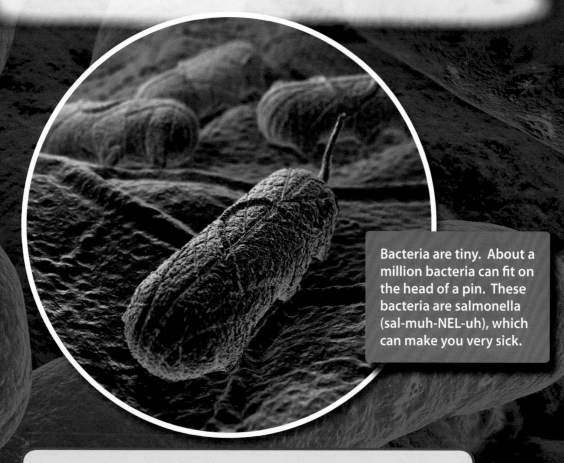

Bacteria are tiny. About a million bacteria can fit on the head of a pin. These bacteria are salmonella (sal-muh-NEL-uh), which can make you very sick.

Algebraic expressions are made up of **terms**. In the term $20w$, the number (20) that is multiplied by the variable is called the **coefficient**. The term $20w$ means "20 multiplied by the value w."

coefficient $\longrightarrow$ $20w$ $\longleftarrow$ variable

Did you know that germs can even be found on soap? Regular soap does not kill germs. It helps to lift the germs off the skin so that those germs may then be rinsed off. You can reduce the number of germs on your soap by rinsing the bar after you use it.

Suppose you wash your hands for 20 seconds, 12 times per day. Evaluate the expression 20w to find the time spent washing your hands each day.

- Identify the expression.   20w

- Identify the value of the variable. $w = 12$

- Substitute.   20(12)

- Evaluate the numerical expression.   240

- Label the answer with the correct
  unit of measure.   240 seconds

You spend 240 seconds washing your hands each day.

The table below shows the expression 20w evaluated for different values of the variable w.

Number of Times Hands are Washed	Expression for Seconds Spent Washing Hands	Total Time Spent Washing Hands (in seconds)
w	20(w)	20w
1	20(1)	20
3	20(3)	60
8	20(8)	160
10	20(10)	200
13	20(13)	260

Each time you wash your hands, try to do it for at least 20 seconds in warm water with soap. Singing the "Happy Birthday" song twice is a good way to estimate that amount of time.

Surgeons (SUR-juhns) must scrub their hands and forearms for two to six minutes before surgery. They must be wearing clean scrub suits, surgical caps, and masks when they "scrub in" before a surgery. While washing, they keep their hands above their elbows so that the dirty water will drip away from their clean hands.

LET'S EXPLORE MATH

a. Dr. Ramirez takes five minutes to scrub in before a surgery. If she scrubs in *s* times per day, write an expression to show how many minutes she spends scrubbing in each day.

b. Evaluate the expression you wrote in problem **a** if Dr. Ramirez scrubs in three times per day.

c. Evaluate the expression you wrote in problem **a** if Dr. Ramirez scrubs in 10 times per day.

Imagine a small hospital that has four surgeons in one department and two surgeons in another department. Each surgeon scrubs in three times per day. An expression can be written to figure out how many total minutes they spend scrubbing in.

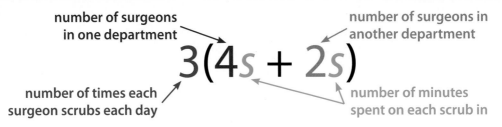

number of surgeons in one department

number of surgeons in another department

$$3(4s + 2s)$$

number of times each surgeon scrubs each day

number of minutes spent on each scrub in

Evaluate the expression when each surgeon scrubs in for six minutes each time. Use the order of operations to evaluate the expression:

- Substitute 6 for *s* $3(4 \cdot 6 + 2 \cdot 6)$

- Work inside the grouping.
  Multiply in order from left to right. $3(24 + 12)$

- Add inside the grouping. $3(36)$

- Find the product of 3 and 36.   108

- Label the answer with the correct unit of measure: 108 minutes

We have found that the surgeons spend a total of 108 minutes each day washing their hands.

Order of Operations

The order of operations gives rules for the order of evaluating expressions.

1. Evaluate inside any *groupings*.
2. Evaluate *exponents*.
3. *Multiply* or *divide* in order from left to right.
4. *Add* or *subtract* in order from left to right.

Some products help kill germs. Bleach, antibacterial soap, hand sanitizer gel, and alcohol wipes are some of these products. A hospital keeps a large stock of these cleaning supplies. Look at the **inventory** of bleach for three of the hospital's departments.

Bleach Inventory

Department	Full Cases of Bleach	Extra Bottles of Bleach
Surgery	4	4
Emergency Room	2	1
Pediatrics	3	5

Use the variable b to represent the number of bottles of bleach in each case.

Surgery: $4b + 4$
Emergency Room: $2b + 1$
Pediatrics: $3b + 5$
Total Bleach Inventory: $4b + 4 + 2b + 1 + 3b + 5$

We can **simplify** the expression for the total bleach inventory by combining **like terms**. Like terms have the same variables and the same corresponding exponents. A **constant** is a value that stays the same. The constants in the expression above are 4, 1, and 5. Numbers are constants, and they are also like terms.

like terms
$$4b + 4 + 2b + 1 + 3b + 5$$
like terms

Simplified expression: $9b + 10$

Germs in Your Mouth

Did you know that germs can live in your mouth, too? Germs in your mouth can cause cavities (KAV-i-teez). Certain bacteria thrive in the environment in our mouths. They eat food left on our teeth. The waste these bacteria make is acid. The acid dissolves the tooth **enamel** (ih-NAM-uhl), the hard covering on the teeth. Cavities are the result of the acid creating holes in the enamel and in the teeth.

Sugar plays a role in creating cavities, but so do starchy foods such as chips and bread. Sticky foods like caramel and gummy candies are especially a problem since the sugar stays on your teeth longer, giving the bacteria plenty to munch on.

Cavities can be painful. A dental filling is needed to repair a tooth that has a cavity.

Did You Know?
Tooth enamel is the hardest substance in the human body.

Toothpaste was first manufactured in tubes by Dr. Washington Sheffield of Connecticut in 1892.

There are many things you can do to fight against the germs that cause cavities. Brushing your teeth with toothpaste that contains fluoride (FLOHR-ahyd) is helpful. Fluoride helps to strengthen tooth enamel. Flossing daily and visiting a dentist twice each year also help prevent cavities.

Suppose three sixth-grade students recently visited a dentist. Unfortunately, they all had cavities. Estella had six times as many cavities as Marcus. Kai had four times as many cavities as Marcus. Look at the table below. How many cavities did the students have altogether?

Student	Number of Cavities
Marcus	x
Estella	$6x$
Kai	$4x$

- Write an expression.

    If there is not a coefficient in front of the variable, then the coefficient is equal to 1.

$x + 6x + 4x$

- Combine like terms to simplify the expression.

$1x + 6x + 4x = 11x$

The simplified expression is $11x$.

The students have $11x$ cavities altogether.

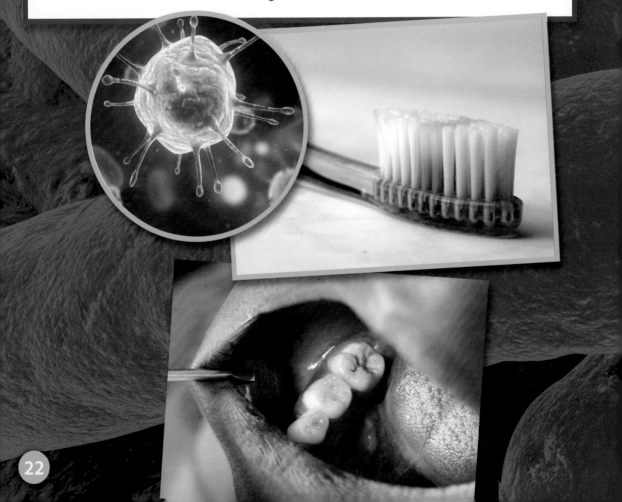

Imagine on their next visit to the dentist, Estella and Kai doubled their number of cavities!

We can find their total number of cavities in two ways. Notice that both methods lead to finding that they have $20x$ cavities. Both methods follow the order of operations.

Method 1: Double the total of both students' cavities:

- Work inside the grouping first. $2(6x + 4x)$
- Multiply. $2(10x)$

     $20x$

Method 2: Double each student's cavities separately:

- Multiply each term by 2. $2(6x) + 2(4x)$
- Add. $12x + 8x$

     $20x$

The Distributive Property

Did you notice that $2(6x + 4x) = 2(6x) + 2(4x)$? We know this is true because of the distributive property. The distributive property states that for all numbers a, b, and c, $a(b + c) = ab + ac$, and $a(b - c) = ab - ac$.

X-rays help a dentist see cavities.

Germs All Around

In a doctor's office or hospital, germs may lurk on used surgical and dental tools. These tools need to be **sterilized** (STER-uh-lahyzd) after they are used so that they are completely free of germs.

An autoclave (AW-tuh-kleyv) is used to sterilize medical tools. It uses pressure and steam combined with extremely high temperatures. Usually, tools are placed in an autoclave for three minutes at a temperature of 273°F (134°C). Not everything can withstand the conditions of an autoclave. For example, many plastics would melt.

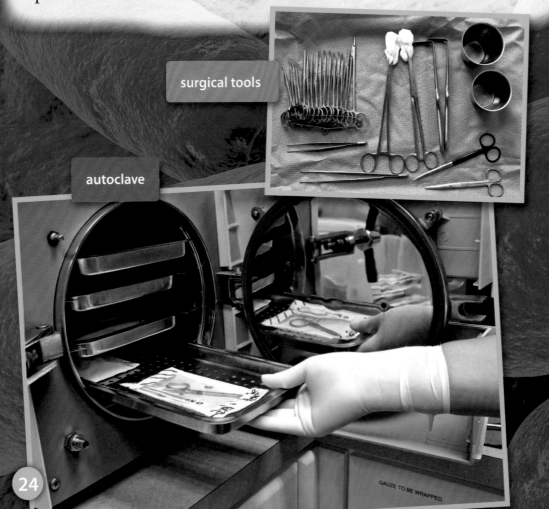

surgical tools

autoclave

GAUZE TO BE WRAPPED

At home, you can get rid of germs without an autoclave. Simply putting an object in a pot of boiling water for several minutes will help eliminate many germs. Other items, like sponges, can be heated in a microwave or dishwasher to kill germs. Surfaces like countertops and bathtubs can be disinfected with bleach or antibacterial wipes.

LET'S EXPLORE MATH

Each week, Jermaine stocks alcohol wipes at the hospital on Mondays, Wednesdays, and Fridays. He stocks x cases on Mondays. On Wednesdays, he stocks 3 times as many cases as he does on Mondays. On Fridays, he stocks double the amount that he stocks on Wednesdays.

a. Write an expression to show the number of cases Jermaine stocks on Wednesdays.

b. Write an expression to show the number of cases Jermaine stocks each Friday.

c. Write an expression to show the total number of cases Jermaine stocks each week. Simplify the expression.

d. Evaluate the expression you wrote in problem **c** when $x = 6$.

Where You Least Expect Them

Which would you rather touch, a toilet seat or a computer keyboard? You probably expect to find germs on a toilet seat. But the average keyboard has more germs than the average toilet seat!

Think of a single key of a computer keyboard. Suppose that key has 100 bacteria cells on it. Imagine those bacteria going through four doublings each hour. After an hour, the key would have 1,600 germs on it!

Evaluating Expressions

$100 \cdot 2^4$	Evaluate this expression to find the number of germs.
$100 \cdot (2 \cdot 2 \cdot 2 \cdot 2)$	Evaluate the exponent. Multiply 2 by itself four times to show four splits.
$100 \cdot (16)$	Multiply the number of bacteria cells by the total number of splits (16).
1,600	Find the value of the expression.

Gross!
Computer keyboards have been found to have 40,000 times more germs than toilets.

LET'S EXPLORE MATH

To help fight germs, a hospital is replacing every computer keyboard. Find the total number of keyboards ordered.

Hint:

Remember the order of operations.

1. Evaluate inside any *groupings*.
2. Evaluate *exponents*.
3. *Multiply* or *divide* from left to right.
4. *Add* or *subtract* from left to right.

a. There are three hospital departments. Each department needs two keyboards for general use and seven for individual use. Write and evaluate an expression to find the total number of keyboards needed.

b. There are 20 computers that are used in the pediatric department. There are two teams of doctors with three doctors on each team who already have new keyboards. Write and evaluate an expression to find the number of new keyboards that are still needed in the pediatric department.

E. Coli Outbreak

A strain of *E. coli* bacteria has contaminated some food and made many people in six towns very sick.

Week 1: Sick Town has reported 60 more cases than Queasy Town.

Week 2: The number of new cases has tripled in Sick Town, Sicker Town, and Sickest Town. Last week, 70, 79, and 81 new cases were reported, respectively.

Week 3: Ailment Town and Unwell Town are now reporting that their number of new cases has increased four times since the first outbreak.

Solve It!

a. Write expressions that show the number of cases reported by Sick Town in weeks 1 and 2, based on the number of cases in Queasy Town.

b. Write an expression that shows the number of cases reported in week 3. Let *a* represent the number of cases first reported by Ailment Town. Let *u* represent the number of cases first reported by Unwell Town.

c. Evaluate the expression you wrote in problem **b** if $a = 30$ and $u = 20$.

d. One *E. coli* bacterial cell divided three times in one hour. Write an expression to represent the number of bacteria after *n* hours. How many would there be after 3 hours?

Use the steps below to help you solve the problems.

Step 1: To solve problem **a**, use *c* to represent the number of cases reported by Queasy Town. For the cases reported in week 1, write an expression to show 60 more than *c*. For the cases reported in week 2, write an expression for three times 60 more than *c*. Simplify the expression.

Step 2: To solve problem **b**, think about what "four times" means.

Step 3: To solve problem **c**, substitute the values in your expression.

Step 4: To solve problem **d**, use exponential form to represent the growth of the bacteria. Use the variable *n* to represent the number of hours. Then evaluate the expression when $n = 3$.

Glossary

algebraic expression—a mathematical phrase that is a combination of one or more numbers and variables, and one or more operations

bacteria—single-celled microorganisms with many, but not all, of the structures found in a typical cell

base—the number used as a factor in exponential form

boiling point—the temperature at which a liquid becomes a gas

coefficient—the number that multiplies a variable; 8 is the coefficient in $8b$

constant—a quantity that always stays the same

contaminated—made impure by mixing with something unclean

enamel—the hard covering of the surface of the tooth

evaluated—found the value of

exponent—a number that tells how many times to multiply a base by itself; in a^b, b is the exponent

exponential form—the form a^b, which shows the number of times (b) that a number (a) is to be multiplied by itself

infections—the presence of disease-causing microorganisms in the body

inventory—a complete listing of stock on hand

like terms—the terms in a mathematical expression that have the same variables and the same corresponding exponents

microbes—living things that can only be seen through magnification, as with a microscope

numerical expressions—mathematical phrases that are a combination of one or more numbers and one or more operations

simplify—to combine like terms and apply mathematical properties to an expression until no further operations can be performed

sterilized—to be made completely free of germs

terms—the parts of an algebraic expression or equation, such as numbers, variables, or combinations of the two

variable—a symbol or letter that represents an unknown value

viruses—microorganisms that do not have a cell wall, cell membrane, or cell nucleus; they must invade other cells in order to stay alive and create more of themselves

Index

Let's Explore Math

Page 10:

a. $192 - 162$

b. $(30)(60)$

c. $19{,}710 \div 365$

Page 13:

a. 5^3

b. 5^6

Page 17:

a. $5s$

b. $5(3) = 15$ minutes

c. $5(10) = 50$ minutes

Page 25:

a. $3x$

b. $2(3x)$

c. $x + 3x + 2(3x) = x + 3x + 6x = 10x$

d. $10x = 10(6) = 60$ cases

Page 27:

a. $3(2 + 7) = 27$ keyboards

b. $20 - 2(3) = 14$ keyboards

Problem-Solving Activity

a. week 1: $c + 60$; week 2: $3(c + 60) = 3c + 180$

b. $4(a + u)$ or $4a + 4u$

c. 200 cases

d. 8^n; 512 bacteria cells